My Country
Ukraine

Annabel Savery

A⁺
Smart Apple Media

Published by Smart Apple Media,
an imprint of Black Rabbit Books
P.O. Box 3263, Mankato, Minnesota 56002
www.blackrabbitbooks.com

Published by arrangement with the Watts Publishing Group
LTD, London.

Library of Congress Cataloging-in-Publication Data
Savery, Annabel. Ukraine / by Annabel Savery.
pages ; cm.—(My country)
Audience: K to grade 3.
Summary: "Anatoliy, a young boy from Ukraine, introduces
readers to his country's landscape, weather, foods, and
festivals. Anatoliy also tells readers about his school,
family life, and things to see in Ukraine. Includes a page of
facts about Ukraine's population, geography, and culture"—
Provided by publisher.
Includes index.
ISBN 978-1-59920-908-1 (library binding)
1. Ukraine—Juvenile literature. I. Title.
DK508.13.S28 2015
947.7—dc23
                 2012042903

Series Editor: Paul Rockett
Series Designer: Paul Cherrill for Basement68
Picture Researcher: Diana Morris

Every attempt has been made to clear copyright. Should
there be any inadvertent omission please apply to the
publisher for rectification.

Picture credits: Slav Bukhai/Shutterstock: 10; Stephen
Coyne/Art Directors/Alamy: 13c; Dmitro2009/
Shutterstock: front cover l; Sergii Figurnyl/Shutterstock:
front cover c, 4c, 9b, 13b, 16b, 18b, 22t; Anton Gvozdikov/
Shutterstock: 2, 19; Hamsterman/Shutterstock: 14;
Ferdinand Hollweek/Alamy: 9c; Idealink Photography/
Alamy: 16c; Thomas Imo/Alamy: 17; joyfull/Shutterstock:
7; Yana Kabagbu/Shutterstock: 15t; Sergey Kamshylin/
Shutterstock: front cover r, 11; Oleksandr Kotenko/
Shutterstock: 8; Alexandra Lande/Shutterstock: 5;
mycola/Shutterstock: 6; Oleg Nikishin/Getty Images:
15b; Olinchuk/Shutterstock: 4bl; Dmitri Ometsinsky /
Shutterstock: 20; pdesign/Shutterstock: 22c; Elena
Pollshchuk/Shutterstock: 18c; Gennadiy Poznyakov/
Alamy: 1, 12; Kostyantyn Sulima/Shutterstock: 24; Lilyana
Vynogradova/Alamy: 21.

Printed in Stevens Point, Wisconsin at Worzalla
PO 1654
4-2014

9 8 7 6 5 4 3 2 1

# Contents

All words in **bold** appear in the glossary on page 23.

Ukraine in the World

My name is Anatoliy, and I live in Ukraine.

• Chernobyl
Kiev •

Dnipropetrovsk •

• Odesa

Ukraine's place in the world.

Striped area on map is claimed by both Ukraine and Russia.

I live in Dnipropetrovsk (say "dnee-proh-peh-trov-szk"), which is a city in eastern Ukraine.

Ukraine is in the continent of Europe. After Russia, Ukraine is the biggest country in Europe.

Many countries border Ukraine. These include Russia, Belarus, Poland, Slovakia, Hungary, Romania, and Moldova.

This is Kiev, the capital city of Ukraine.

Ukraine's Landscape

This machine is used for harvesting crops.

Much of the land in Ukraine is open **steppe**. This is flat grassland where farmers can raise animals.

The soil is rich and **fertile**, which means it is very good for growing crops, such as **grain** and vegetables. The land also has large areas covered by thick forest.

In 1986, a disaster occurred at the Chernobyl **nuclear power plant** in the north of Ukraine.

The disaster left the ground around the site **contaminated** by **radioactive** material.

This is the nuclear power plant at chernobyl. It has been many years since the disaster, but people are not allowed to live near it.

The Weather in Ukraine

Much more rain falls throughout the year in the north and west than in the south and southeast.

Winters are very cold with a lot of snow.

It can snow a lot in the carpathian mountains in eastern Ukraine.

Summers in Ukraine are warm. It is very hot in the south, and many people go on vacation to the Black Sea coast.

Ukraine's coast includes Crimea, an area recently claimed by Russia.

I like to go to the beach and swim in the sea.

People Who Live in Ukraine

Ukraine's **ancestors** have come from all over the world.

Many people in Ukraine come from other European countries, such as Russia and Turkey.

Ukraine was once part of Russia. Many people speak both Ukrainian and Russian.

Religious buildings are beautifully decorated. Religion is very important in Ukraine and most people are Christians. You can see churches in most towns.

This is Saint Sophia Cathedral in Kiev.

At Home with My Family

I live with my mom, dad, grandmother, and my big brother, Aleksandr. We call our grandmother "Baba."

Families are very important to people in Ukraine.

In Ukraine, many **generations** live together in one house.

Our family has a house in the city and also a house in the country, which is called a dacha.

It has a big garden, and we grow fruit and vegetables.

Many families have a second home in the countryside.

Our dacha is lots of fun in the summer. I like to help in the garden.

What We Eat

Borscht is a soup made from vegetables, including beetroot.

History has taught people in Ukraine how important food is. The country has had several famines.

We eat lots of soups and stews made with vegetables and herbs. The most famous is borscht.

Another of the national foods is *salo*, which is **cured** pork fat.

People like to eat *salo* with bread as a snack.

Mom is very proud of her cooking and likes to invite people over for dinner.

People love to eat together and share food and drink tea.

Going to School

I go to an elementary school. This is the school for children ages 6 to 10. My brother, Aleksandr, is in the lower secondary school, which has children from 10 to 15.

All children attend school until they are 15.

School is fun! When I grow up, I want to be a pilot.

When Aleksandr leaves school, he can choose to go to an upper secondary or a vocational school.

The vocational school will teach him to do a particular job.

young people study at upper secondary schools go to a university.

Festivals and Celebrations

We celebrate many days in Ukraine.

New Year's Eve is a very popular holiday. We decorate a New Year tree and give each other presents.

Easter also is an important holiday. We celebrate with lots of eating and singing.

For Easter, we decorate eggs in bright colors.

Easter is my favorite holiday. What's yours?

On August 24, we celebrate Independence Day. This is in honor of the day in 1991 when Ukraine became independent from the **Soviet Union**.

Things to See

There are many exciting places to visit in Ukraine.

I like visiting the Khotyn Fortress. It was built to defend the country from enemy attacks.

The Khotyn Fortress is 1,000 years old!

My auntie is going to take us to visit the Sofiyivka Park. It is the famous National **Dendrological Park**. It is a beautiful garden where plants and trees are studied.

The National Dendrological Park has lots of special trees and places to explore.

Here are some facts about my country!

Fast Facts about Ukraine

Capital city = Kiev

Population = 44.9 million

Currency = Ukraine Hryvnia (UAH)

Area = 222,098 square miles
(587,450 km²)

Crimea (a disputed territory with Russia) = 10,038 square miles
(26,100 km²)

Main language = Ukrainian, many people also speak Russian

National holiday = Independence Day, August 24

Main religion = Ukrainian Orthodox

Longest river = Dnieper, also known as Dnipro, 1,420 miles
(2,285 km)

Highest mountain = Hora Hoverla, 6,762 feet (2,061 m)

Glossary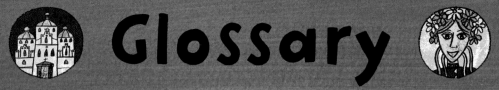

ancestor a person you are related to, who lived a long time ago

cure to salt, smoke or dry meat or fish so it will keep for a long time

contaminated to make dirty, unusable or dangerous

Dendrological Park a place where trees and shrubs are studied

famine a lack or shortage of food in a large area for a long time

fertile soil that is good for growing crops

generations layers of family that are born one after the other, such as grandparents, parents and children

grain wheat, barley, and rye

nuclear power plant a place where power is created using nuclear reactions

radioactive material that gives off radioactive energy which can damage living things

Soviet Union country made up of Russia, Ukraine and other neighboring countries

steppe a large area of flat grassland without trees

Further Information

Websites

usa.mfa.gov.us (Ukraine Embassy in the U.S.)

www.mamalisa.com/?t=ec&p=984&c=152

Book

Van Cleaf, Kristin. *Ukraine (The Countries)*. ABDO Pub. Co., 2008.

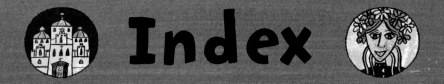

Index